Potato Cookbook

Tantalize Your Taste Buds with Delicious Potato Treats

We all have been living with a general misconception that potatoes are unhealthy, fattening, and not fit for people who are diet conscious and we could not have been more wrong. Potato is packed with nutrients and is a food that is best for consumption for people who are calorie conscious. Potatoes are a rich source of dietary fibers, manganese, potassium, copper, vitamin C, vitamin B6 and much more. This is the reason why we have compiled for you fifty nutrient rich potato recipes that will help you incorporate healthy potato dishes in your diet. This eBook includes:

1. Fifty mouth watering and healthy potato recipes.
2. Cooking time so that you can easily plan your schedule.
3. Serving size to give you a fair idea about how many people can enjoy the delicious meals.
4. Nutrition information so that you can keep count of the calories.
5. Recipes for appetizers, breakfast, lunch and dinner.

Read along and see how you can use potatoes to enhance the taste of your meals and to make each meal nutrient rich. Try out these recipes and enjoy the tasty delight with your family and loved ones.

Contents

Introduction - Top 5 Advantages of Eating Potatoes

Potatoes are not only tasty but they are also loaded with numerous health benefits. They are excellent sources of minerals, vitamins, and fibers that play a role in improving the health of the heart and protecting the body against cancer. Following are the five major benefits that you will get by adding potatoes in your meals:

Reduction in Inflammation

Potatoes are nightshade and wholesome vegetables that are packed with Vitamin C, niacin, calcium, protein, and carbohydrates. They are easy to digest because they are rich in fiber and contain vitamin C, which helps in repairing the cells of the body and also function as anti oxidants. They help in relieving the inflammation in the digestive track and intestines.

Enhanced Brain Function

Our brain needs balanced levels of Omega-3, amino acids, Vitamin B complex, oxygen, glucose and other fatty acids to function at its maximum capacity. Potatoes contain all these elements so they help in enhancing the performance of the brain.

Prevention of Heart Diseases

Potatoes are rich in Vitamin C and B complex, niacin, calcium, protein and carbohydrates. All these nutrients help control blood pressure levels and fight against heart diseases. They also contain carotenoids which are essential for the health of the heart and overall wellness and health of a human body.

Prevention of Kidney Stones

Potatoes are rich in magnesium which can limit the accumulation of calcium in kidneys, hence preventing kidney stones.

Skin Care

Potatoes have all the nutrients that are essential for the health of your skin. They contain phosphorus, zinc, magnesium, potassium, Vitamin C and B complex that are very good for your skin. Raw potatoes can also be applied to the skin to relive pain, soreness, or swelling.

These are only some of the many health benefits of potatoes so add them in your diet today and experience a positive change in your overall health and wellness.

Appetizers

Baked Potato Wedges with Delicious Dip
Serves 8

Cooking time 10 minutes

Nutritional Information (per serving): Calories 353, Total Fat 24g, Protein 11g, Carbohydrates 23g

Crispy potato wedges with a delicious dip containing taco seasoning which is a perfect appetizer.

Ingredients

Black olives (sliced and drained) 2.25 ounces

Tomatoes (chopped) ½ cup

Cheddar cheese 1 cup

Cilantro (fresh and chopped0 2 tbsp

Sour cream 1 cup

Softened cream cheese 8 ounces

Taco seasoning 1.25 ounces

Olive oil 2 tbsp

Potato wedges 2 packs

Directions

Heat the oven to 450 degree Fahrenheit.

Use a non-stick cooking spray to grease a baking pan of 15x10x1 inches.

Drizzle olive oil on potato wedges and toss until the wedges are properly coated.

Add 2 tbsp taco seasoning in potato wedges and toss again to mix.

Transfer potatoes on the baking pan and place the pan in the pre-heated oven.

Bake for about 15 to 20 minutes and flip once so that the wedges are crisp and golden brown from both sides.

Meanwhile mix the remaining taco seasoning, cilantro, sour cream, and cream cheese together. Whisk until all the ingredients are well incorporated.

Spread the mixture on a serving platter and top it with olives, tomatoes, and cheese.

Serve with warm potato wedges.

Crunchy Fries

Serves 5

Cooking time 1 hour and 10 minutes

Nutritional Information (per serving): Calories 145, Total Fat 7g, Protein 2g, Carbohydrates 19g

Crispy and delicious baked potato fries.

Ingredients

Vegetable oil 1 tbsp

Potato slices 2 cups

Celery seed ¼ tsp

Salt 1 tsp

Honey 2 tsp

Melted butter 2 tbsp

Pepper sauce (cayenne) 2 tbsp

Directions

Heat the oven to 425 degree Fahrenheit.

Mix celery seed, salt, honey, melted butter, and cayenne pepper sauce in a bowl.

Add sliced potatoes in the mixture and toss until potatoes are evenly coated.

Allow it to rest for 5 minutes.

Pour vegetable oil in a baking pan and spread potato slices in it.

Place the baking pan in oven and bake for about 30 to 35 minutes. Flip potatoes once and allow them to turn golden brown.

Potato and Shrimp Puffs

Serves 5

Cooking time 35 minutes

Nutritional Information (per serving): Calories 50, Total Fat 2g, Protein 7g, Carbohydrates 1g

Soft potato and shrimp puff that will melt inside your mouth.

Ingredients

Mango chutney 9 oz

Baby shrimps 8 oz

Eggs 4

Curry powder 2 tbsp

Massed potatoes 24 oz

Directions

Chop the shrimps and mix with curry, potatoes, and eggs.

Make small puffs from the mixture and fry until they turn golden brown.

Serve puffs with mango chutney and enjoy.

Cheese, Potato and Ham Puffs

Serves 16

Cooking time 50 minutes

Nutritional Information (per serving): Calories 123, Total Fat 6g, Protein 4g, Carbohydrates 13g

Delicious combination of cheese, ham, and potatoes for an incredible side dish

Ingredients

Refrigerated biscuits 16.3 oz

Cumin (ground) ¼ tsp

Sour cream 2 tbsp

Cheese (shredded) ½ cup

Ham (diced) ½ cup

Water 1 tbsp

Potatoes (diced) 1 cup

Onion (diced) ½ cup

Directions

Heat the oven to 350 degree Fahrenheit.

Chop potatoes and place them in a microwavable bowl with water. Cover the bowl and microwave on high for about 3 to 4 minutes or until the potatoes are soft. Remove the bowl from oven and drain water.

In bowl mix cumin, sour cream, cheese, ham, onion, and cooked potatoes and combine well.

Take out the biscuits from the pack and separate the halves. Place biscuit in a 3 ½ circles and use a tablespoon to place a generous amount of mixture in the center of each biscuit. Fold the biscuits to cover the filling and press the edges together to seal them shut.

Take an ungreased baking sheet and place the biscuits on it. Bake for about 10 to 12 minutes or until the puffs turn golden brown.

Potato Poppers with Jalapeno

Serves 24 poppers

Cooking time 1 hour 15 minutes

Nutritional Information (per 3 poppers): Calories 213, Total Fat 8g, Protein 6g, Carbohydrates 29g

Spicy, sizzling and crispy potato poppers

Ingredients

Cooking spray (butter flavored)

Crumbs of cornflakes 3 cups

Eggs (large) 3

Green onions (chopped finely) 1/3 cup

Mashed potatoes with cream cheese and jalapeno 2 cups

Directions

Heat the oven to 400 degree Fahrenheit.

Mix 1 egg, green onions and mashed potatoes in a bowl until all the ingredients are well incorporated. Form 1 inch balls of the entire mixture.

Place crumbs in a bowl.

Whisk the remaining 2 eggs in a bowl with 2 tbsp of water in a separate bowl.

Roll potatoes in crumbs, then in egg mixture and back in crumbs until the poppers are nicely coated.

Place poppers in a baking sheet lined with foil and lightly coated with cooking spray.

Bake poppers for about 15 to 20 minutes or until browned and crisp.

Potatoes with Nacho Toppings

Serves 4

Cooking time 1 hour

Nutritional Information (per serving): Calories 414, Total Fat 22g, Protein 28g, Carbohydrates 25g

Potato wedges served with nacho toppings to serve as a perfect appetizer.

Ingredients

Sour cream

Black olives (chopped) ¼ cup

Green onions (chopped) ¼ cup

Tomato (chopped) 1 cup

Lettuce (chopped) 1 ½ cup

Salt ½ tsp

Salsa sauce 1 cup

Beef (ground) 1 lb

Taco seasoning 1 tbsp

Olive oil 1 tbsp

Potato wedges 3 cups

Directions

Heat the oven to 450 degree Fahrenheit.

Grease a baking pan with non stick cooking spray.

Mix potato wedges with taco seasoning and oil and toss to combine well.

Place potatoes in the prepared baking sheet and bake for about 15 to 20 minutes or until the wedges are crisp ad brown.

Meanwhile, cook beef in a non-stick skillet until it is cooked through and brown. Add salt and salsa sauce,

Divide potatoes wedges in 4 serving plates followed by one fourth meat mixture.

Generously garnish each serving with 1 tbsp olives, 1 tbsp green onions, ¼ cup tomatoes, 1/3 cup lettuce, followed by sour cream.

Serve and enjoy.

Potatoes with Parmesan

Serves 4

Cooking time 30 minutes

Nutritional Information (per serving): Calories 117, Total Fat 4g, Protein 5g, Carbohydrates 14g

Simple and delicious potato wedges topped with parmesan cheese.

Ingredients

Salt ¼ tsp

Garlic powder ½ tsp

Parmesan cheese ¼ cup

Olive oil 1 tbsp

Potato wedges 3 cups

Directions

Heat the oven to 425 degree Fahrenheit and grease a baking dish with cooking spray.

In a bowl mix olive oil and potatoes and spread on the baking sheet.

Sprinkle parmesan cheese, salt and garlic powder over potatoes on each side.

Bake

Pot Stickers Filled With Cheese and Potatoes

Serves 40 pot stickers

Cooking time 1 hour 40 minutes

Nutritional Information (per serving): Calories 53, Total Fat 2g, Protein 1g, Carbohydrates 6g

Crispy pot stickers with delicious potato filling

Ingredients for pot stickers

Wraps for pot stickers 12 oz

Green onions (chopped) 2 tbsp

Bell peppers (red and chopped) 3 tbsp

Cheddar cheese (shredded) 1/3 cup

Mashed potatoes 2 cups

Ingredients for Water

Vegetable oil 3 to 4 tbsp

Ingredients for Dipping Sauce

Sesame seeds 1 tsp

Sesame oil 1 tsp

Soy sauce ½ cup

Directions

Mixed green onions, red pepper, cheese, and mashed potatoes in a bowl.

Place pot sticker wraps on the working surface and place 2 tsp of potato mixture in the middle of each wrap. Brushes the edges of pot stickers with water and fold in half like a half moon. Press edges to seal shut.

Heat oil in a non-stick skillet over medium flames and swirl pan to cover the base of skillet with oil. Transfer pot stickers in skillet and cook for 2 to 3 minutes on each side until light golden.

Continue cooking pot stickers in the same way until the entire mixture is used.

Meanwhile, mix all the ingredients of sauce in a bowl and serve as a dipping sauce with pot stickers.

Potato Chips

Serves 6

Cooking time 25 minutes

Nutritional Information (per serving): Calories 44, Total Fat 5g, Protein 2g, Carbohydrates 12g

Crunchy potato chips with a slight twist of spices to tickle your taste buds.

Ingredients

Potato wedges 1 pack

Garlic powder 1/8 tsp

Paprika ¼ tsp

Thyme leaves (dried) ¼ tsp

Salt ½ tsp

Directions

Mix garlic powder, paprika, thyme, and salt together in a bowl and let it stand aside.

Heat oil to 370 degree Fahrenheit in a deep and large saucepan.

Add half of the potato wedges in hot oil and cook for about 5 to 8 minutes, turning them occasionally.

Carefully remove the cooked wedges from the saucepan and use a paper towel to drain the excess oil. Sprinkle half of the seasoning mixture on the cooked potato wedges.

Repeat the frying process with the rest of the potato wedges and serve with the dip of your choice.

Potato Wedges with Cheese Fondue

Serves 6

Cooking time 50 minutes

Nutritional Information (per serving): Calories 499, Total Fat 30g, Protein 25g, Carbohydrates 25g

Enjoy baked potato wedges with a creamy cheese fondue.

Ingredients

A dash of black pepper

Juice of lemon 1 tbsp

Halved clove of garlic (large) 1

Apple juice (unsweetened) 1 ½ cups

Cornstarch 2 tbsp

Shredded Swiss cheese 2 cups

Shredded Gouda cheese 3 cups

Potato wedges 1 pack

Olive oil 1 tbsp

Directions

Heat the oven to 425 degree Fahrenheit.

Coat potato wedges in oil and place them on a baking sheet and roast until golden brown or crisp for about 20 to 25 minutes.

In the mean time mix cornstarch and cheese in a large bowl and place it aside.

Rub a garlic clove on the inside of a fondue pot or a sauce pan of medium size.

Heat apple juice in that sauce pan over medium flames until the juice starts to simmer. Reduce the heat and add cheese in the sauce pan in small portions, until the cheese melts completely.

Serve roasted potatoes with the mixture of cheese and enjoy.

Roasted Spicy and Sizzling Potatoes

Serves 6

Cooking time 50 minutes

Nutritional Information (per serving): Calories 278, Total Fat 2g, Protein 7g, Carbohydrates 63g

Spicy potatoes that will make your mouth water.

Ingredients

Cayenne pepper ¼ tsp

Salt ¼ tsp

Paprika ¼ tsp

Sugar ¼ tsp

Garlic salt ½ tsp

Onion powder ½ tsp

Chili powder 1 tsp

Vegetable oil 1 tbsp

Potato wedges 1 pack

Directions

Heat the oven to 425 degree Fahrenheit.

Coat potato wedges in oil and keep aside.

Take a small bowl and mix all the remaining ingredients in it and add the seasoning in potato wedges.

Toss to coat the wedges completely and place them on a baking sheet.

Bake until light brown for about 25 to 30 minutes.

Serve with a dip of your choice.

Hash Brown with Spinach and Goat Cheese

Serves 6 (2 each)

Cooking time 45 minutes

Nutritional Information (per serving): Calories 147, Total Fat 14g, Protein 4g, Carbohydrates 3g

Perfect assortment of cheese, spinach and hash browns

Ingredients

Eggs (medium) 2

Whole milk 4 tbsp

Goat cheese 6 tbsp

Garlic powder 1/8 tsp

Salt to taste

Tomatoes (chopped) 1 tbsp

Spinach 2 cups

Lemon pepper ¼ tsp

Salt 1 tsp

Olive oil 5 tbsp

Hash browns (shredded) 1 pack

Directions

Heat the oven to 400 degree Fahrenheit.

Mix hash browns with lemon pepper, oil and salt in a bowl until all the ingredients are well incorporated.

Use cooking spray to grease a muffin tin tray.

Place a tablespoon of hash brown mixture in every muffin cup and press in the center to form a shape of a bowl. Place the muffin tin tray in the pre heated oven and bake for about 20 to 25 minutes.

Remove the tray from oven and allow it to rest.

Reset the oven to 375 degree Fahrenheit.

Meanwhile, sauté spinach in 1 tablespoon olive oil for about 6 to 8 minutes. Add garlic powder, salt, and tomatoes in spinach and cook for 2 more minutes over medium flames.

In a separate bowl mix milk and goat cheese until the mixture is creamy and smooth.

Beat eggs in a separate bowl with a dash of salt and add spinach and goat cheese mixture in it. Mix until all ingredients are well incorporated.

Place the egg mixture in the center of the baked hash browns and bake for about 15 minutes at 400 degree Fahrenheit.

Carefully remove from the tray and enjoy.

Breakfast

Crispy and Crunchy Hash Browns

Serves 4

Cooking time 20 minutes

Nutritional Information (per serving): Calories 413, Total Fat 19.5g, Protein 4.7g, Carbohydrates 54.8g

An easy to cook and delicious recipe of hash browns that you can use with just about anything.

Ingredients

Salt to taste

Pepper to taste

Grated potatoes 1 pound

Olive oil 3 tablespoon

Directions

Use a large sauce pan to heat oil over medium heat.

Squeeze the excess moisture from the grated potatoes and add them in the heated oil. Spread the potatoes evenly at the base of the sauce pan.

Sprinkle pepper and salt over the potatoes and cook until golden brown. Flip to cook from the other side and continue to cook until hash browns are golden brown from both sides and properly cooked through

Yummy Egg Rolls

Serves 30 rolls

Cooking time 1 hour 15 minutes

Nutritional Information (per egg role): Calories 174, Total Fat 6g, Protein 8g, Carbohydrates 21g

Yummy rolls filled with hash browns and eggs.

Ingredients

Melted butter 3 tbsp

Water 3 tbsp

Roll wraps 2 packs

Cheddar cheese (shredded) 2 cups

Hash browns 3 cups

Lightly beaten eggs (whole) 8

Sausages 1 pack

Directions

Preheat the oven to 450 degree Fahrenheit.

Use a non-stick skillet to cook sausages until they start turning brown. Drain extra grease from the sausages and place them in a large bowl.

Cook eggs in the same skillet over medium to low heat. Once scrambled mix it with hash browns, sausages, and cheese in a large mixing bowl until all the ingredients are well incorporated.

Take an egg roll wrap and place it on work surface. Place 2 tablespoon potato mixture on the bottom of the egg wrap keeping one inch margin and start folding. Lightly brush the edges with water. Press the edges of the wrap to seal the roll. Repeat the process with the remaining egg roll wraps and filling.

Place rolls on a cookie sheet and brush it with melted butter.

Bake in the preheated oven for about 11 to 14 minutes until the rolls turn golden brown.

Egg with Hash Brown

Serves 4

Cooking time 30 minutes

Nutritional Information (per serving): Calories 347, Total Fat 39g, Protein 19g, Carbohydrates 28g

A complete, healthy and delicious breakfast with eggs and potatoes

Ingredients

Pepper

Salt

Dijon mustard 2 tsp

Sour cream ½ cup

Hash browns (shredded) 3 cups

Vegetable oil 3 tbsp

Red onion (chopped) ½ cup

Sausages 1 lb

Eggs (whole) 4

Directions

Use a non stick skillet to cook onion and sausages over medium heat until sausages starts turning brown. Remove onion and sausages from skillet and drain the excess grease.

Cook hash browns according to the recipe mentioned above. Cook potatoes about 7 minutes on each side, or until both the sides are golden brown.

Mix mustard, sour cream, onion, and sausages in a bowl until all the ingredients are well incorporated. Add mixture to the skillet with hash brown and cook until all the ingredients are heated through.

Divide the mixture in four serving plates, and top each plate with a fried or poached egg.

Quick Breakfast

Serves 8

Cooking time 15 minutes

Nutritional Information (per serving): Calories 293, Total Fat 19g, Protein 17g, Carbohydrates 14g

A unique and yummy combination of potatoes and eggs, perfect for a great start of the day

Ingredients

Chopped onions (green)

Cheddar cheese (shredded) 1 cup

Milk 1 cup

Lightly beaten eggs (whole) 8

Chopped onions 1 cup

Cubed ham (cooked) 1 cup

Hash browns 3 cups

Olive oil 3 tbsp

Directions

Heat oil in a non-stick skillet over medium heat and add hash browns, onions, and ham in it. Cook for about 8 to 10 minutes or until potatoes start turning golden brown. Use salt and pepper to add taste.

Mix milk and slightly beaten eggs in a bowl and add in the skillet. Reduce flame and continue cooking with occasional stirring until still moist but starts to set.

Remove the skillet from heat and garnish with shredded cheese. Allow the cheese to melt and then sprinkle chopped green onions to decorate.

Shepherd's Pie

Serves 6

Cooking time 45 minutes

Nutritional Information (per serving): Calories 477, Total Fat 31g, Protein 23g, Carbohydrates 28g

The classic recipe of shepherd's pie with a yummy twist

Ingredients

Cheddar cheese (shredded) 1 cup

Beef hash (coned) 1 can

Jalapeno (chopped) ¼ cup

Onion powder 1 tbsp

Paprika 1 tbsp

Chopped bell pepper (red) 1 cup

Potatoes (diced) 3 cups

Olive oil 2 tbsp

Pepper

Salt

Feta cheese (crumbled) ¼ cup

Eggs 6

Chopped garlic clove 1

Chopped onion (green) ¼ cup

Bacon 6 slices

Directions

Heat the oven to 350 degree Fahrenheit and grease a baking sheet.

Use a large skillet to cook bacon over medium flames until it turns crispy. Use a paper towel to drain extra grease. Crumble the slices of bacon into small pieces.

Reserve 1 tbsp grease from bacon in skillet and add garlic and onion in it and cook for about 1 to 2 minutes over medium heat or until onion is soft and tender.

Use a fork to beat egg in a bowl and add pepper and salt to season. Add garlic, onion, bacon, and feta cheese in eggs and mix well.

Transfer the mixture in the greased baking sheet and bake in the pre heated oven for about 20 minutes.

In the mean time use a large skillet to heat olive oil. Add chiles, bell pepper, and diced potatoes in the heated oil. Cook for about 12 minutes or until the potatoes turn tender with occasional stirring. Use onion powder, paprika, salt and pepper to season.

Take a small saucepan and heat beef hash in it.

When the eggs are properly baked, spread corned beef over the baked eggs evenly followed by the potato mixture.

Sprinkle cheese on top.

Return the baking dish in oven for about 5 minutes until all the layers are set and the cheese melts.

Creamy Hash Browns in a Cup

Serves 12

Cooking time 40 minutes

Nutritional Information (per serving): Calories 165, Total Fat 9g, Protein 9g, Carbohydrates 11g

A cup full of delicious flavors of sausages and potatoes

Ingredients

Cheddar cheese (shredded) ½ cup

Italian seasoning (dried) ½ tsp

Lightly beaten eggs (whole) 8

Chopped bell pepper (red) ¼ cup

Mushrooms (chopped) ½ cup

Sausages (ground) ½ lb

Salt ¼ tsp

Melted butter ¼ cup

Hash browns 3 cups

Directions

Pre heat the oven to 400 degree Fahrenheit.

Combine salt, butter, and hash browns in a bowl and divide the mixture in 12 greased muffin tin cups. Place the muffin tin tray in the preheated oven and bake for about 12 to 15 minutes or until the edges starts turning golden.

In the mean time, use a 10 inch skillet to cook Italian sausages until brown, add bell pepper and mushrooms in the skillet. Cook until the vegetables turn tender. Divide the sausage mixture on top of the baked hash browns.

Mix seasoning and eggs in a bowl and pour the mixture over the sausage and hash brown layers in the muffin cup followed with cheese on top.

Again place the muffin tin tray in the pre heated oven and bake for about 12 to 14 minutes or until all the layers are properly cooked through.

Potatoes with Corned Beef

Serves 4

Cooking time 20 minutes

Nutritional Information (per serving): Calories 351, Total Fat 4g, Protein 14g, Carbohydrates 34g

A delicious combination of potatoes and corned beef served with poached or fried eggs to add to the taste.

Ingredients

Skim milk (evaporated) ¼ cup

Canola oil 2 tbsp

Ketchup ¼ cup

Chopped bell pepper (green) 1 tsp

Garlic (chopped) 1 tsp

Chopped corned beef (cut into ½ inch pieces) ½ lb

Diced potatoes 2 cups

Onion (diced) ½ cup

Eggs (whole) 4

Directions

Combine ketchup, garlic, pepper, beef, potatoes, and onions in a large mixing bowl.

Use a non-stick skillet to heat oil over medium flames.

Transfer the potato mixture in the skillet and spread it evenly at the base of the skillet and cook for about 10 minutes without stirring.

Turn potatoes and cook for about 7 to 8 minutes from the other side until the potatoes are cooked and tender.

Turn down the heat to low and slowly add skimmed milk with light constant stirring. Cook for another minute or until all the ingredients are properly cooked through.

Serve with a fried or poached egg.

Diced and Seasoned Potatoes

Serves 4

Cooking time 16 minutes

Nutritional Information (per serving): Calories 116, Total Fat 4g, Protein 3.03g, Carbohydrates 26.2g

Simple yet delicious recipe of potatoes that you can enjoy with any dip of your choice or even serve as a side dish

Ingredients

Salt

Pepper

Vegetable oil 2 tbsp

A dash of red chilies

Diced potatoes

Directions

Heat vegetable oil in a non stick skillet over medium heat.

Add diced potatoes in a bowl and add salt, pepper, and chili to taste and toss to evenly coat the potatoes. You can add any more seasonings if you like.

Add the potatoes in skillet and cover the lid. Cook for about 7 to 8 minutes. Remove the lid only to turn the potatoes after every 3 to 4 minutes.

Easy To Cook Vegetable Frittata

Serves 4 to 6

Cooking time 25 minutes

Nutritional Information (per serving): Calories 225, Total Fat 12.1g, Protein 17.08g, Carbohydrates 13.7g

Creamy, healthy, and delicious vegetable frittata that you can enjoy at breakfast

Ingredients

Cheddar cheese (shredded) 1 cup

Milk ¼ cup

Eggs (medium) 6

Garlic pepper ¼ tsp

Salt 1 tsp

Chopped bell pepper 9red) ½ cup

Chopped zucchini (medium) 1

Diced potatoes 3 cups

Onion (chopped) 1 cup

Olive oil 2 tbsp

Directions

Use a nonstick skillet to heat oil in it. Add pepper, salt, bell peppers, zucchini, potatoes, and onions in heated oil. Cook for about 2 minutes with constant stirring.

Turn down the heat to low and cook with occasional stirring for about 8 to 10 minutes on until the vegetable turn soft and tender.

Beat eggs in a bowl with milk and salt. Pour the egg mixture over the vegetables in the skillet and cover the skillet with lid. Allow to cook for about 10 minutes or until the eggs are starting to set.

Pre heat the broiler and place the skillet in it. Broil for about 2 minutes or until the eggs are completely set and the top of the eggs is browned and set.

Drizzle shredded cheese on top and broil for another minute to melt the cheese.

Slice into triangular wedges before serving.

Potato Pancakes

Serves 6

Cooking time 20 minutes

Nutritional Information (per serving): Calories 309, Total Fat 25g, Protein 5g, Carbohydrates 17g

Crispy pancakes that you can enjoy in breakfast or as a side dish at dinner.

Ingredients for Pancakes

Pepper ¼ tsp

Salt 1 tsp

Chopped onions ¼ cup

Beaten eggs (medium) 3

Hash browns 3 cups

Ingredients for Dill Sauce

Salt ½ tsp

Dill weed (dried) ½ tsp

Chopped chives (fresh) 1 tbsp

Mayonnaise ½ cup

Sour cream ½ cup

Directions

Mix all the ingredient of dill sauce in a small bowl until all the ingredients are well blended. Cover the bowl and place in the refrigerator until it is time to serve.

Mix pepper, salt, onions, eggs, and hash browns in a bowl.

Use a non-stick skillet to heat 1 tbsp oil over medium flames. Place 1/4th of the potato mixture in the skillet for one pancakes and spread it slightly towards the base of the skillet.

Cook potatoes for about 3 to 4 minutes on both sides or until they are golden brown.

Repeat the process with the remaining mixture.

Garnish pancakes with dill sauce to serve.

Hash Brown Crispy Cups with Mushrooms and Italian Sausage

Serves 12

Cooking time 35 minutes

Nutritional Information (per serving): Calories 147, Total Fat 9g, Protein 9g, Carbohydrates 7g

A perfectly delicious combination of sausages, eggs, and potatoes that you can enjoy anytime you like.

Ingredients

Cheddar cheese (shredded) ½ cup

Italian seasoning (dried) ½ tsp

Lightly beaten eggs (whole) 8

Chopped bell pepper (red) ½ cup

Mushrooms (chopped) ½ cup

Sausages ½ lb

Salt ¼ tsp

Melted butter ¼ cup

Hash browns 3 cups

Directions

Heat the oven to 400 degree Fahrenheit.

Grease a regular muffin tin tray and place aside.

Mix salt, melted butter, and hash browns in a medium bowl until all the ingredients are well incorporated.

Place about 1/4 cup of potato mixture into each muffin cup and place the muffin tin tray in the oven and bake for about 12 to 15 minute or until the potatoes starts turning golden brown.

In the mean time cook ground sausages in a skillet and drain excess grease. Add pepper and mushrooms in skillet and cook with occasional stirring until the vegetables turn soft and tender. Place the sausage mixture in the muffin cups.

In a bowl combine eggs with Italian seasoning until all the ingredients are well incorporated. Four the egg mixture equally into each muffin cup and top it with shredded cheese.

Bake for about 12 to 14 minutes or until all the layers are set and properly cooked through.

Cheese and Potato Spanish omelet

Serves 4

Cooking time 35 minutes

Nutritional Information (per serving): Calories 171, Total Fat 6g, Protein 11g, Carbohydrates 18g

A healthy and fulfilling omelet for a perfect breakfast

Ingredients

Cheese (shredded) ¼ cup

Egg whites 1 ¼ cups

Pepper

Garlic salt ½ tsp

Chopped tomatoes 1/3 cup

Ham (chopped) ½ cup

Chopped bell pepper (green) 1/3 cup

Hash brown 2 cups

Onions (chopped) ½ cup

Olive oil 1 tbsp

Directions

Use a non-stick skillet to heat oil over medium flames. Add bell peppers, onions, and potatoes in the skillet and cook for about 10 to 12 minutes or until the vegetable are soft and tender, with occasional stirring. Add pepper, garlic salt, tomatoes, and ham to the skillet.

Pour the beaten egg whites over the ingredients in the skillet and top it with shredded cheese.

Stir gently to combine all the ingredients.

Cover the skillet and cook until all the ingredients are set for about 8 minutes.

Transfer the omelets on the serving plate and slice into wedges to serve.

Lunch

Sizzling Potato Tacos

Serves 6

Cooking time 50 minutes

Nutritional Information (per serving): Calories 150, Total Fat 9g, Protein 2g, Carbohydrates 16g

Spicy sizzling tacos, served with a twist

Ingredients

Taco shells 6

Chopped jalapeno 1

Chopped garlic 1

Onion (chopped) 1 cup

Oil 2 tbsp

Potatoes 1 ½ lb

Lime, cilantro, and pepper jack (all shredded) for garnishing

Directions

Place potatoes in a pot with cold water. Cover the pot and bring to boil. Boil until the potatoes are tender. Drain the water and break up.

Use a nonstick skillet to heat oil and add jalapeno, garlic, and onion in the oil and cook for about 3 minutes.

Add potatoes in the skillet and season. Spread the mixture at the base of the skillet and cook for about 9 minutes.

Serve the mixture in taco shells.

Dosas with Chickpea and Potato Filling

Serves 4

Cooking time 1 hour

Nutritional Information (per serving): Calories 120, Total Fat 3g, Protein 2g, Carbohydrates 17g

Indian style Dosas perfect for a yummy treat

Ingredients for Filling

Cold water 1 ¾ cups

Vegetable oil 1/3 cup

Turmeric (ground) ½ tsp

Cinnamon (ground) ½ tsp

Curry powder 1 tbsp

Smashed cloves of garlic 3

Ginger (fresh, peeled and chopped in 2 ½ inch pieces) 1

Jalapeno (chopped with seeds) 1

Cumin seeds 2 tsp

Coconut flakes (unsweetened) 1/3 cup

Potatoes 1 ½ lb

Cilantro (fresh and chopped) ½ cup

Peas (frozen) ½ cup

Chickpeas (drained and rinsed) 1 can

Chopped onion 3 cups

Salt 1 tsp

Ingredients for Dosas

Cold water 2 cups

Salt ½ tsp

Cumin seeds ½ tsp

Flour (all purpose) ½ cup

Rice flour ½ cup

Semolina flour ½ cup

Vegetable oil

Directions for Filling

After the peeling the potatoes chop then into 1 ½ inch pieces. Soak potatoes in a bowl with enough cold water to cover all the potatoes.

Use a medium sized nonstick skillet to toast coconut flakes with occasional stirring for about 3 minutes or until they turn golden. Transfer the flakes to a bowl.

Toast cumin seeds in the same skillet after wiping it clean. Stir the seeds for about 30 seconds until they are darker in shade and fragrant. Transfer the seeds to a separate small bowl.

Blend garlic, singer and jalapeno with salt, ¼ cup water, oil, turmeric, cinnamon, and curry powder until all the ingredients are well blended and form a smooth paste. Transfer the paste to the skillet and cook with constant stirring for about 1 minute or until the paste starts to thicken. Add onions in the paste and cook until onions are softened.

Drain the water of the potatoes and add in the skillet. Add cumin seeds in the skillet and cook for about 10 minutes or until the potatoes are tender, with occasional stirring.

Add remaining 1 ½ cup water and chickpeas in the skillet. Cook for about 15 to 20 minutes until the potatoes are soft and tender.

Add peas in the skillet and cover it to cook for 3 more minutes.

Remove the mixture from heat and top it with cilantro and toasted flakes of coconut.

Direction for Dosas

Add salt, cumin seed, flours and water in a bowl.

Add oil in a 12-inch skillet and place it over medium flames. Transfer ½ cup of the flour mixture in the skillet and swirl it to spread it across the base of the skillet. Allow it to cook until the edges starts to turn golden for about 2 minutes. Flip Dosa carefully with the help of a rubber spatula ad cook the upper side for 1 more minute. Transfer to the plate.

Cook with the remaining batter and stack them in a plate. Cover with a foil to keep them warm.

Place the filling in dosa and serve while hot.

Jacket Potatoes

Serves 4

Cooking time 1 hour 40 minutes

Nutritional Information (per serving): Calories 353, Total Fat 8.5g, Protein 12.60g, Carbohydrates 41g

Jacket potatoes with a delicious filling of meat and carrots

Ingredients

Peas (frozen) ½ cup

Chopped carrots (roasted) 1 cup

Basil (fresh and chopped) ½ cup

Pepper

Salt

Oregano (dried) 1 tsp

Tomato sauce 3 cups

Tomato paste 1/3 cup

Garlic (crushed) 3 cloves

Chopped onions (brown) ½ cup

Mince (beef) 1 kg

Potatoes (large) 4

Parmesan cheese (grated) to garnish

Directions for Mince Mixture

Use a deep frying pan to heat 1 tbsp oil over medium flames. Add mince in it in batches until it is browned. Place in a bowl.

Add the remaining oil in the pan and add onions in it. Cook onions for about 3 minutes or until they turn soft. Add garlic and cook for another minute. Add mince in pan and add tomato paste in the pan. Stir to mix well. Add dried oregano and tomato sauce in the pan and bring it to boil.

Turn down the heat to low and add pepper and salt to season. Allow the mixture to simmer for about 30 minutes with occasional stirring. Remove the pan from heat and add basil in the mixture.

Allow it to cool for about 15 minutes.

Directions for Potatoes

Heat the oven to 200 degree centigrade.

Wash and dry the potatoes and pierce all over with the help of a fork.

Wrap each potato in a foil and place them on a baking sheet. Bake for about 1 hour and 20 minutes. Remove from oven and keep them aside.

Transfer the mince mixture in a pan over medium heat. Add carrot in the mixture and allow boiling. Add ¼ cup of water if necessary.

Turn down the heat and simmer for about 10 minute. Add peas in and simmer until the peas turn tender for about 5 more minutes. Add pepper and salt to season.

Remove the potatoes from the foil carefully and cut a cross in the center of each potato.

Squeeze the base of the potatoes gently to open up the top. Place potatoes on a serving plate and fill the top with mine mixture.

Serve hot.

Delicious Hasselback Potatoes

Serves 4

Cooking time 45 minutes

Nutritional Information (per serving): Calories 451, Total Fat 11g, Protein 15g, Carbohydrates 68g

A delicious and healthy choice for a perfect lunch

Ingredients

Parmesan (grated) ¼ cup

Breadcrumbs ½ cup

Salt to taste

Dash of cayenne pepper

Paprika (smoked) 2 tsp

Olive oil 2 tbsp

Large peeled potatoes (halved) 8

Directions

Heat the oven to 200 degree centigrade.

Place a potato on your work surface and cut it side down and make cuts on its surface at approximately 5 mm intervals. Place it in a bowl and repeat the process with the remaining potatoes.

Drizzle oil over the potatoes and season with cayenne and paprika. Sprinkle pepper and salt to taste and toss the bowl to coat all the potatoes evenly. Transfer the potatoes to roasting pan.

Place the pan in the preheated oven for about 30 minutes and flip the potatoes once to cook properly from both sides.

In the meantime mix parmesan and breadcrumbs in a bowl. Remove potatoes from oven and turn them so that the cut side in down.

Sprinkle the cheese mixture over the potatoes and place them back inside the oven. Bake the potatoes about 15 to 20 minutes or until they are crisp and golden brown.

Serve right out of oven.

Pumpkin and Potato Bake

Serves 4

Cooking time 50 minutes

Nutritional Information (per serving): Calories 521, Total Fat 20g, Protein 29g, Carbohydrates 18g

A delicious combination of pumpkins and potatoes

Ingredients

Cheese (grated) 1 cup

Thyme 2 tbsp

Eggs (medium) 6

Chicken corn soup 300g can

Drained corns 270g can

Pumpkin (deseeded and peeled, chopped into 1 ½ cm cubes) 750g

Peeled potatoes (chopped into 1 ½ cm cubes) 750g

Directions

Heat the oven to 200 degree centigrade.

Grease an ovenproof dish with a 10 cup capacity.

Place pumpkin and potatoes in separate plates that are microwave safe. Drizzle both with 2 tbsp water and use a plastic wrap to cover the plate and microwave both on high heat for 3 minutes or until pumpkin and potatoes are tender. Transfer both to the greased dish and add corn. Stir to mix.

Transfer soup in a jug and add thyme and egg in it. Use pepper and salt to season. Use a form to beat the mixture until all the ingredients are well incorporated.

Pour the soup and egg mixture over the vegetables. Sprinkle cheese on top.

Bake for about 45 to 50 minutes or until the pumpkin and potatoes are cooked through.

Serve.

Perfect Potato Pizzas

Serves 8

Cooking time 2 hours and 5 minutes

Nutritional Information (per serving): Calories 243, Total Fat 10g, Protein 5g, Carbohydrates 31g

Easy to cook individual pizzas

Ingredients

Thyme leaves 2 tbsp

Peeled potatoes 500g

Olive oil 1/3 cup

Water (lukewarm) 200ml

Salt 1 tsp

Yeast 8g

Sifted flour 1 cups

Directions

Use a large mixing bowl to mix salt, yeast, and flour. Pour water in the center of the mixture with 1 tbsp oil. Mix well until the mixture takes a dough form.

Grease your hands with oil and knead the dough on your work space. Knead until the dough springs back when pressed for about 5 minutes. Place the dough in a large bowl and keep it aside for an hour or until it has doubled in size.

Heat the oven 220 degrees.

Press the dough down and slice into 8 even slices. Give an oval shape to all the 8 pieces about 1 cm thick.

With the help of a slicer cut really fine slices of potatoes. Pat them dry using a paper towel and place on the dough in a single layer slightly overlapping each other.

Sprinkle thyme and season with pepper and salt. Drizzle oil on each pizza dough and bake in the oven for about 15 to 20 minutes or until the dough is golden and crisp.

Serve fresh out of oven.

Gnocchi

Serves 4

Cooking time 1 hour 30 minutes

Nutritional Information (per serving): Calories 434, Total Fat 4g, Protein 16g, Carbohydrates 79g

Bite size and cheesy gnocchi to enjoy at lunch

Ingredients

Parmesan (grated) ¼ cup

Four (plain) 2 cups

Lightly beaten egg 1

Ground pepper (white) to taste

Salt to taste

Peeled and quartered potatoes 4

Flour (plain) to dust

Directions

Add water in a saucepan up to 3 cm and bring it to boil. Place potatoes in a steaming basket and place in the sauce pan while making sure that it does not touch the water.

Steam the potatoes until tender or for about 5 minutes. Transfer steamed potatoes to a bowl and mash with the help of a masher until smooth and season with pepper and salt.

Add egg in potatoes and mix with a wooden spoon until well combined. Add half of the parmesan and flour in the mixture and mix well. Add the rest of the flour in 2 batches and combine until firm dough is formed. Place the mixture on a floured surface and knead using your hands.

Use a baking paper to line a baking sheet. Divide the dough into equal portions and roll each portion into a log that 30 cm long and 2 cm in width. Use a knife to cut 2 cm pieces of dough from each log.

Flour your hands lightly and form a ball of each piece of dough. Roll each ball over a fork and place on a tray.

Bring salted water to boil in a saucepan and one quarter of the prepared gnocchi in the pan and cook until they rise to the surface for about 3 minutes. Drain with the help of a slotted spoon and transfer to a bowl.

Cover the bowl with foil to keep gnocchi warm.

Smoked Trout with Potato Rosti

Serves 4

Cooking time 45 minutes

Nutritional Information (per serving): Calories 297, Total Fat 12g, Protein 18g, Carbohydrates 29g

Delicious combination of trout and dill served on potatoes

Ingredients

Smoked trout 250g

Baby rocket 50g

Vegetable oil 2 tbsp

Peeled potatoes 800g

Ingredients for Dill Cream

Lemon juice 2 tbsp

Sour cream 2 tbsp

Chopped capers (drained) 2 tsp

Dill sprigs (chopped) 2 tbsp

Gherkins (chopped) 2

Directions

With the help of a vegetable peeler, peel the potatoes into thin slices. Squeeze to drain excess moisture.

Use a large frying pan to heat oil over medium flames. Add quarter of the potato slices in oil and use a spatula to flatten them at the base of the frying pan and cook for about 3 to 4 minutes.

Line a plate with paper towels and transfer the cooked potatoes on it to drain extra grease.

Cook the remaining potatoes in the same way.

In the mean time prepare the dill cream. Mix lemon juice, sour cream, capers, dill, and gherkin in a mixing bowl.

Transfer potatoes on a serving plate followed by trout and baby rocket.

Garnish with dill mixture before serving.

Tasty Tortilla with Potatoes

Serves 8

Cooking time 1 hour 10 minutes

Nutritional Information (per serving): Calories 171, Total Fat 6g, Protein 11g, Carbohydrates 18g

A an appetizing and filling lunch recipe packed with taste and nutrition

Ingredients

Black pepper

Salt

Eggs (medium0 8

Finely sliced, peeled potatoes 3

Crushed cloves of garlic 4

Halved onion (finely sliced) 1

Speck (chopped into 2 cm pieces)

Olive oil ¼ cup

Directions

Take a 30cm frying pan and heat 1 tablespoon of oil in it. Add garlic, onion, and speck in the pan and cook until the onions are soft and tender for about 10 minutes.

Take out the mixture in a bowl.

Heat the rest of the oil in the pan and add potatoes in it. Cook for about 25 minutes until the potatoes are soft and golden brown.

Heat the grill on high. Whisk eggs in a bowl and use pepper and salt to season the eggs.

Add onion in the potatoes and pour the eggs over onions and potatoes. Shake the pan to allow the eggs to reach the base of the pan.

Cook over medium flames until the tortilla is set and golden for about 8 minutes.

Place tortilla in the preheated oven, 6 cm away from the heat and cook until it is set and golden for 5 minutes.

Lose the edges of tortilla with the help of a knife and allow cooling for 5 minutes.

Slice in wedges before serving.

Healthy Potato Salad

Serves 4

Cooking time 25 minutes

Nutritional Information (per serving): Calories 276, Total Fat 3.30g, Protein 10.60g, Carbohydrates 48g

Simple yet delicious potato salad

Ingredients

Shredded basil leaves ½ cup

Chopped Ham 100 grams

Olive oil

Onion (chopped) 1

Lemon juice 1

Mayonnaise 1 cup

Potatoes (chopped into 2 cm cubes)

Directions

Place potatoes in a sauce pan with cold water, cover and bring the water to boil. Reduce heat and cook for 3 to 4 more minutes or until the potatoes are soft and tender. Drain the potatoes and place them in a bowl.

Mix salt, onion, 2 tbsp lemon juice, and mayonnaise in a small mixing bowl. Transfer half of the mixture to boiled potatoes and stir gently with the help of a plastic spatula. Cover the bowl with a plastic wrap and place it aside.

Spray olive oil in a non-stick frying pan and heat it over medium flames. Cook ham in it until it is golden brown or for about 3 to 4 minutes. Allow it to cool.

Add the remaining mayonnaise mixture, basil, and ham in the potatoes and stir to until all the ingredients are well incorporated.

Use pepper and salt to season and serve.

Cheesy and Creamy Mashed Potatoes

Serves 4

Cooking time 45 minutes

Nutritional Information (per serving): Calories 304, Total Fat 16g, Protein 11.3g, Carbohydrates 27g

Creamy potato mash that you can enjoy with just about anything

Ingredients

Parmesan (grated) ½ cup

Breadcrumbs (fresh) ¼ cup

Onions (finely sliced) 2

Cheese blend 1 cup

Warm milk ¼ cup

Chopped butter 40 grams

Potatoes (peeled and chopped) 800 grams

Directions

Fill a sauce pan with water and place potatoes in it. Bring the water to boil over high flames and cook until potatoes are tender for about 10 to 15 minutes. Drain and keep aside.

Place potatoes in a pan over medium heat. Toss until all the excess moisture is gone. Transfer to a bowl and mash until they form a smooth paste. Add in green onions, cheese blend, milk and butter and mix until all the ingredients are well incorporated.

Grease a baking dish and preheat the grill on medium heat. Transfer the mash in the greased baking sheet and smooth it with the help of a spatula. Sprinkle breadcrumbs on top and use pepper to season it. Grill the mash until it is golden brown or for about 5 to 10 minutes.

Serve.

Potatoes, Spinach and Chicken Bake

Serves 6

Cooking time 1 hour 40 minutes

Nutritional Information (per serving): Calories 531, Total Fat 28g, Protein 24g, Carbohydrates 44g

Delicious combination of chicken, potatoes and sweet potatoes baked in layers of tasteful delight

Ingredients

Butter 60 grams

Cooked spinach (drained and chopped) 100 grams

Shredded and roasted chicken ½ large

Sliced mushrooms 200 grams

Crushed garlic 1 clove

Chopped onions 1

Chopped bacon 4

Olive oil 1 tablespoon

Sweet potatoes (halved and peeled) 500 grams

Potatoes (medium) 1 kg

Butter (melted) to serve

Parmesan (grated) ¾ cup

Milk 3 cups

Flour (plain) ¼ cup

Broccolini (steamed) for garnishing

Directions

Fill a sauce pan with water and place sweet potatoes and potatoes in it to boil. Cook potatoes for about 15 to 20 minutes or until they are soft and tender and drain extra water. Peel and slice sweet potatoes are potatoes.

In the mean time use a prying pan to heat half of the oil over medium flames. Cook onion and bacon in it for about 5 minutes. Transfer both the bowl and pour the rest of the oil in the pan. Cook mushrooms in the pan until they are soft and tender or for about 3 to 5 minutes. Add mushrooms to the bowl and add in spinach and chicken in it.

Use a saucepan to melt butter until it is foaming over medium heat. Add flour in the butter and cook for about 2 to 3 minutes or until the ingredients starts to bubble. Remove the pan from heat and add milk in it gradually.

Place the back on medium flames and stir until a thick sauce is formed. Add 2/3 of the parmesan in the mixture and use pepper and salt to season it. Add the mixture to the bacon mixture reserving around 1 cup of the sauce.

Use melted butter to grease a freeze proof baking dish. Place potatoes over the base slightly overlapping each other. Place half the chicken mixture and sweet potatoes on top of it. Top it with another layer of potatoes, sweet potatoes and rest of the chicken. Garnish with the reserved sauce on top. Use a plastic wrap to cover the dish and place it in the freezer over night.

Before serving, preheat the oven to 200 degree Centigrade. Sprinkle the remaining parmesan on top and bake in the oven for about 50 minutes or until it turn golden.

Garnish with Broccolini.

Tasty Patty Sticks

Serves 12 sticks

Cooking time 40 minutes

Nutritional Information (per serving): Calories 194, Total Fat 6.2g, Protein 4.5g, Carbohydrates 9.6g

Delicious potato patties that you can enjoy with any dip of your choice

Ingredients

Lemon juice (fresh) 2 tbsp

Cilantro (chopped) 2 tbsp

Salt

Pepper 1 tsp

Dinner role (stale) 1

Potatoes (medium) 3

Oil

Directions

Boil potatoes in a sauce pan.

Allow them to cool before peeling and mashing them in a bowl. Soak the stale dinner roles in water and squeeze the excess water out. Crush the dinner role and add it in the potatoes.

Add lemon juice, cilantro, salt, and pepper in the mixture and mix well until all the ingredients are well incorporated. Divide the mixture into 12 portions and use your hands to give it the form of cylindrical sticks.

Use a non stick pan to heat oil and place 4 potato stick in it at a time. Cook the sticks properly until it is golden brown on all sides. Repeat the process with the remaining sticks and serve with the sauce of your choice.

Dinner

Delicious Potato Gratin

Serves 8

Cooking time 1 hour 15 minutes

Nutritional Information (per serving): Calories 587, Total Fat 40g, Protein 18g, Carbohydrates 40g

A meal filled with the richness of potatoes, cheese and milk that will keep you from putting your spoon down

Ingredients

Gruyere (shredded) 3 cups

Pepper (ground)

Potatoes (large) 4

Salt to taste

Cream 2 cups

Milk 2 cups

Peeled garlic (large) 4

Butter 2 tbsp

Directions

Great a 2 quart dish for casserole with butter and rub 1 garlic clove on the insides of the dish and then discard the clove.

Mix remaining garlic, salt, cream, and milk in a saucepan over medium flames. Bring the mixture to boil and then turn down the heat and allow simmering for about 5 minutes. Remove garlic cloves from the mixture and discard.

Heat the oven to 350° Fahrenheit. In the mean time, peel the potatoes and rinse them. Use a paper towel to dry potatoes and then chop into thick slices of 1/8 inches.

Place the potatoes at the base of the casserole dish, overlapping each other.

Pour ¼ cup of the mixture of milk, followed by ¾ cup of shredded cheese, salt, and pepper. Repeat the layers (reserving about ½ cup of shredded cheese) until layers reach ½ inch from the brink of the casserole dish.

Garnish with a layer of cheese on top.

Line a baking sheet with foil and place the casserole dish on that. Bake until the cheese is brown, and the casserole starts to bubble for about 30 to 45 minutes. Remove the dish from oven and allow cooling for about 10 to 12 minutes.

Potato and Leek Gratin

Serves 12

Cooking time 1 hour 15 minutes

Nutritional Information (per serving): Calories 290, Total Fat 18g, Protein 5g, Carbohydrates 30g

A delicious combination of leeks and potatoes layered with delicious milk and cream

Ingredients

Chopped parsley (fresh) ¼ cup

Milk 1 cup

Heavy cream 2 cups

Sliced garlic 4 cloves

Leeks 10 (washed, medium sized leeks with light green and white part only. halved vertically and chopped horizontally into 1 inch pieces)

Butter (unsalted) 2 tbsp plus more for greasing the dish

Potatoes (small) chopped into 1/8 thick slices

Salt to taste

Directions

Heat the oven to 375° Fahrenheit.

Use a large pot to boil potatoes in salted water for 5 minutes. Drain the potatoes well and keep aside.

Use a large skillet to heat butter and sauté garlic and leeks in butter for about 7 minutes or until the vegetables are tender and keep aside.

Use a 9x13 inch baking dish and grease it with butter. Arrange half of the potatoes at the base of the dish overlapping each other. Top the layer with ½ cup milk and 1 cup cream and a dash of salt followed by leeks. Arrange the rest of the potatoes on top and pour the rest of the milk and cream over potatoes and sprinkle with salt to taste.

Place the dish in the preheated oven until the top turn golden brown, potatoes are soft and tender, and the milk and cream have been properly absorbed by the potatoes and leeks for about 45 minutes.

Use parsley to garnish before serving.

Roasted Turnips and Potatoes

Serves 8

Cooking time 1 hour 30 minutes

Nutritional Information (per serving): Calories 367, Total Fat 22.7g, Protein 12.6g, Carbohydrates 29.6g

A delicious mixture of potatoes and bacon served with the goodness of turnip

Ingredients

Butter (unsalted) 2 tbsp

Minced garlic (fresh) 1 tsp

Pepper 1 tsp

Salt 1 ½ tsp

Minced rosemary (fresh) 1 tbsp

Heavy cream ½ cup

Potatoes (medium) 4diced into 1 inch pieces

Turnips (small) 4 diced into ½ inch pieces

Bacon ½ pound

Directions

Heat the oven to 400° Fahrenheit.

Use a saucepan to cook bacon over medium flames. Drain the saucepan reserving some drippings and chop bacon into 1 inch pieces.

Place bacon in a large bowl with drippings. Add garlic, pepper, salt, rosemary, cream, potatoes, and turnip and toss to combine all the ingredients.

Take a shallow baking dish and transfer the mixture in it. Top the mixture with butter and use a foil to cover.

Bake in the preheated oven for about 50 minutes. Remove the covering of the dish and allow it to bake for 25 more minutes until the top is brown and the vegetables are soft and tender.

Serve fresh out of oven.

Potato and Ham Gratin

Serves 8

Cooking time 1 hour 20 minutes

Nutritional Information (per serving): Calories 312, Total Fat 17g, Protein 13.5g, Carbohydrates 26g

Perfect combination of ham and potatoes baked in ramekins for more taste in every portion

Ingredients

Half and half 1 ½ cups

Chopped parsley (fresh) 2 tbsp

Gruyere (grated) 1 ¼ cups

Cubed ham (glazed) 1 ½ cup

Potatoes (peeled and cut in fine slices) 2 lbs

Fresh pepper (ground) ½ tsp

Salt ¾ tsp

Finely sliced onions (medium) 1

Butter (unsalted) 2 ½ tbsp plus more to grease the ramekins

Directions

Heat the oven to 325° Fahrenheit.

Use a medium sized skillet to melt butter over medium flames. Add onions in the skillet and season it with ¼ teaspoon of pepper and salt each. Cook for about 25 minutes or until the onions turn translucent and deep brown.

Remove the onions from heat and mix with parsley, cheese, ham, and potatoes. Use pepper and salt to season.

Take 8 ramekins and use butter to grease them. Evenly divide the potato mixture in 8 ramekins and top each ramekin with 3 tbsp of half and half followed by rest of the butter.

Use a foil to cover each ramekin and place in the preheated oven for about 30 minutes. Remove the foil and bake until potatoes are soft and tender for 35 more minutes.

Remove from oven and allow cooling for 5 minute before serving.

Potato Dumpling and Chicken Soup

Serves 6

Cooking time 55 minutes

Nutritional Information (per serving): Calories 122, Total Fat 3g, Protein 3g, Carbohydrates 22g

Yummy soup with the added flavor of potato dumplings

Ingredients for Dumplings

Chopped parsley (fresh) 1 tbsp

Milk 3 tbsp

Baking mix (all purpose) 1 cup

Mashed potatoes 1 cup

Ingredients for Soup

Seasoning (Italian) ½ tsp

Bay leaf 1

Chicken (cooked and chopped) 2 cups

Chicken broth 3 cans

Onions (chopped) ½ cup

Carrots (sliced) 1 cup

Vegetable oil 1 tbsp

Directions

Mix all the dumplings ingredients in a bowl and combine well until all the ingredients are well incorporated and keep the bowl aside.

Use a skillet to heat oil and add onions, celery and carrots in it. Cook onions with occasional stirring for about 6 to 8 minutes or until the vegetables are soft and tender. Add Italian seasoning, bay leaf, chicken, and chicken broth in the skillet and bring to boil.

Turn down the heat and allow it to simmer until the vegetables are tender for about 10 minutes.

Allow the soup to boil again and divide the mixture of dumplings into 12 balls and add dumpling in soup. Cook without covering for 20 more minutes on low heat. Cover the skillet and cook for 10 more minutes.

Serve hot right out of the pot.

Tasty Soup with Sweet Potatoes

Serves 6

Cooking time 25 minutes

Nutritional Information (per serving): Calories 191, Total Fat 6g, Protein 5g, Carbohydrates 31g

A delicious soup of sweet potatoes with the hint of chicken flavor to enhance the taste

Ingredients

Cumin (ground) ½ tsp

Thyme leaves (dried) 1 tsp

Chicken broth 1 cup

Milk (whole) 1 cup

Mashed sweet potatoes 3 cups

Onions (chopped) ½ cup

Olive oil 1 tbsp

Directions

Use a large saucepan to heat oil. Add onion in it and cook with occasional stirring until onions are soft and tender for about 7 minutes.

Add all the ingredients in the sauce pan and cook for 15 more minutes until all the ingredients are well incorporated.

Pour half of the mixture in a blender and process until it turns smooth. Repeat with the remaining mixture and return the blended mixture to the sauce pan. Cook over low flames until the mixture is properly cooked through.

Serve fresh out of pot and enjoy.

Potato and Leek Soup

Serves 4

Cooking time 45 minutes

Nutritional Information (per serving): Calories 442, Total Fat 33g, Protein 17g, Carbohydrates 20g

Creamy richness of potato soup packed with the taste of leeks and chicken stock

Ingredients

Cayenne sauce ½ tsp

Salt ½ tsp

Chopped chives (fresh) 1 tbsp

Cheddar cheese (shredded) 1 cup

Softened cream cheese (chopped) 3 oz

Heavy cream ½ cup

Milk (whole) 1 cup

Potatoes (chopped) 2 cups

Chicken stock 14 oz

Minced garlic (fresh) 1 tsp

Chopped leeks 1 cup

Chopped bacon 2 slices

Butter 1 tbsp

Directions

Melt butter in a saucepan over medium flames. Add garlic, leeks, and bacon in the saucepan. Cook until bacon is crispy with occasional stirring. Drain grease and add potatoes and chicken broth in the saucepan.

Bring the mixture to boil. Turn down the flames and cook without covering until the potatoes are soft and tender, for 20 to 25 minutes with occasional stirring.

Pour the mixture in the blender and process until it form a smooth puree. Return the blended mixture to the saucepan.

Add all the remaining ingredients in the mixture and cook on low flames until all the ingredients are properly cooked through and well incorporated.

Serve hot and enjoy.

Cheesy Hash Brown with Barbecued Chicken

Serves 4

Cooking time 45 minutes

Nutritional Information (per serving): Calories 470, Total Fat 20g, Protein 36g, Carbohydrates 36g

Easy to cook dish that you can have in the oven in about 10 minutes. Delicious chicken pieces baked with hash browns to make a delicious combination.

Ingredients

Barbecue sauce ¾ cup

Halved chicken breasts (skinless and boneless) 4

Olive oil 2 tbsp

Pepper ¼ tsp

Salt ½ tsp

Onions (chopped) ½ cup

Cheddar cheese (shredded) 1 cup

Hash browns 3 cups

Directions

Preheat the oven to 400 degree Fahrenheit.

Use a nonstick cooking spray to grease a glass baking dish.

Place onions, cheese, and potatoes in the baking dish and season with pepper and salt and drizzle olive oil on top. Toss to combine all the ingredients. Spread the potatoes at the base of the baking dish to cover the bottom of the dish.

Arrange chicken pieces on top of potatoes and pour barbecue sauce on top.

Bake without covering until the potatoes are golden brown and crisp and the chicken pieces are no longer pink.

Potato Skillet with Garlic Chicken

Serves 4

Cooking time 30 minutes

Nutritional Information (per serving): Calories 284, Total Fat 7g, Protein 30g, Carbohydrates 23g

Easy to cook and delicious chicken and potato wedges with only 5 ingredients

Ingredients

Potato wedges 3 cups

Soup mix with herbs and garlic 1 pack

Water 2 cups

Chicken breasts (skinless and boneless) 1 lb

Vegetable oil 1 tbsp

Directions

Use a 10 inch skillet to heat oil. Add chicken and cook until brown from both sides.

In a mixing bowl combine soup mix in water and mix until well incorporated. Add potatoes and soup mixture in skillet and cook with occasional stirring for 13 to 15 minutes or until the potatoes are soft and tender and the chicken pieces are no longer pink.

Serve fresh out of pot and enjoy.

Cheesy Potatoes with Grilled Chicken

Serves 4

Cooking time 45 minutes

Nutritional Information (per serving): Calories 480, Total Fat 26g, Protein 40g, Carbohydrates 20g

The delicious taste and aroma of grilled chicken cooked with potato wedges for a perfect dinner

Ingredients

Black pepper ¼ tsp

Salt 1 tsp

Parmesan cheese ½ cup

Ranch dressing ½ cup

Potato wedges 3 cups

Basil leaves (dried) ½ tsp

Salt (seasoned) ½ tsp

Olive oil 2 tsp

Chicken breasts (skinless and boneless) 4

Directions

Prepare the grill and heat it to medium heat.

Cut 18x12 inch (4 pieces) of aluminum foil and grease 1 side of it with a non-stick cooking spray.

Coat chicken pieces with basil, salt, and olive oil and place it in the center of each piece of aluminum foil.

In a bowl mix the rest of the ingredients making sure the potato wedges are evenly coated. Divide the potato mixture on each piece of foil with chicken. Fold the foil in a way to allow space for the circulation of hot air within each pack.

Grill the packet over medium heat for about 20 minutes. Allow the moisture to escape from the packets by slightly opening the top of the pack.

Grill open packets for 10 more minutes or until the potato wedges are soft and tender and the chicken is no longer pink.

Potato and Chicken Casserole

Serves 6

Cooking time 40 minutes

Nutritional Information (per serving): Calories 194, Total Fat 6.2g, Protein 4.5g, Carbohydrates 9.6g

Packed with the taste of cheese, onion, and bacon; a perfect dinner dish with delicious chicken and potatoes

Ingredients

Onions (green) ¾ cup

Cheddar cheese (shredded) 2 ½ cup

Cooked bacon (crumbled) ¾ cup

Chopped chicken (cooked) 2 cups

Pepper to taste

Salt to taste

Onion (diced) ½ cup

Potatoes 6 cups

Paprika 1 tbsp

Chopped garlic 6 cloves

Olive oil 2 tbsp

Sauce for Buffalo wings 1/3 cup plus 2 tbsp

Directions

Heat the oven to 425 degree Fahrenheit. Grease a baking dish with a cooking spray.

Mix garlic, oil, and 1/3 cup of hot pepper on a large mixing bowl. Add potatoes and mix until the potatoes are well coated.

Spread the potatoes in an even layer in the baking dish and bake for about 20 to 25 minute until the potatoes are tender and crisp with occasional stirring.

Mix the rest of the hot sauce with chicken pieces. Once the potatoes are ready, place a layer of ½ cup cheese on them followed by bacon, chicken and the remaining cheese.

Place the baking dish back in oven and bake for 15 more minutes or until the cheese starts to bubble and melts.

Remove the dish from oven and garnish with green onions before serving.

Potatoes with Pesto and Roasted Chicken

Serves 8

Cooking time 55 minutes

Nutritional Information (per serving): Calories 291, Total Fat 16g, Protein 25g, Carbohydrates 11g

A perfectly baked combo of chicken and potatoes that is good to eat and easy to cook

Ingredients

Chicken pieces (fried) 1 pack

Black pepper ½ tsp

Garlic salt ½ tsp

Crushed rosemary (dried) 1 tbsp

Basil with pesto (refrigerated) ¼ cup

Onions (diced) ½ cup

Potatoes (diced) 3 cups

Directions

Heat the oven to 400 degree Fahrenheit. Spray a baking dish with cooking spray.

Mix pesto, onions, and potatoes with pesto and spread the potatoes are the base of the prepared baking dish.

In a bowl mix pepper, salt, and rosemary until all the ingredients are well incorporated. Rub this mixture over the pieces of chicken and place the chicken n top of the potatoes.

Bake without covering the dish for about 40 to 45 minutes or until the chicken is properly cooked through.

Potato and Chicken Delicious Dinner

Serves 6

Cooking time 30 minutes

Nutritional Information (per serving): Calories 297, Total Fat 12g, Protein 24g, Carbohydrates 23g

Potato wedges with corn and chicken served with sour cream

Ingredients

Sour cream

Cheddar cheese (shredded)

Drained kernel corn 1 can

Water ¼ cup

Potato wedges 3 cups

Chicken breast (diced into 1 inch pieces) 1 lb

Olive oil 2 tbsp

Directions

Use a nonstick skillet to heat oil on medium flames. Add chicken in the skillet and cook until the chicken is no longer punk in the center.

Add water and potatoes in the skillet and cover it. Cook potatoes for about 7 to 8 minutes or until they are tender and golden. Add more water of necessary.

Add corn and salsa in the skillet. Continue to cook until all the ingredients are cooked through and heated. Garnish with cheese and cover the skillet until the cheese melts.

Serve with a scoop of sour cream.

Conclusion

Potatoes not only taste good but they are also rich in nutrients essential for a healthier lifestyle. Potato is the world's most popular vegetable and is loved by both children and adults. Therefore, adding it in your diet whether as a side dish or a main course is the best way to ensure that your children and your family are eating healthy.

In this book you will find fifty different recipes to cook potatoes which will give you plenty of ideas on how to add it in your diet in a healthy yet delicious manner. So try out these recipes today and we bet that you, your family, and your children will love each and every dish.

Made in the USA
Charleston, SC
13 August 2015